Real is the Word They Use to Contain Us

Real is the Word
They Use to Contain Us

NOAH WARENESS

BIBLIOASIS
WINDSOR, ONTARIO

FIRST EDITION

Library and Archives Canada Cataloguing in Publication

Wareness, Noah, author
     Real is the word they use to contain us / Noah Wareness.

Poems.
Issued in print and electronic formats.
ISBN 978-1-77196-159-2 (softcover).--ISBN 978-1-77196-160-8 (ebook)

     I. Title.

PS8645.A7567R43 2017   C811'.6   C2016-907963-5
                                               C2016-907964-3

Edited by Zachariah Wells
Copy-edited by Daniel Wells
Typeset by Chris Andrechek
Cover art and design by Noah Wareness

Canada Council **Conseil des Arts**
for the Arts **du Canada**

ONTARIO ARTS COUNCIL
CONSEIL DES ARTS DE L'ONTARIO
50 YEARS OF ONTARIO GOVERNMENT SUPPORT OF THE ARTS
50 ANS DE SOUTIEN DU GOUVERNEMENT DE L'ONTARIO AUX ARTS

Canadian   Patrimoine
Heritage   canadien

Published with the generous assistance of the Canada Council for the Arts and the Ontario Arts Council. Biblioasis also acknowledges the support of the Government of Canada through the Canada Book Fund and the Government of Ontario through the Ontario Book Publishing Tax Credit.

Noah Wareness works without government funding. All the money he makes from sales of this edition will be donated to a family shelter in his neighborhood. Visit noahwareness.com if you want to read more of his stuff.

PRINTED AND BOUND IN CANADA

MIX
Paper from
responsible sources
FSC® C004071
www.fsc.org

for Daniela
the weirdest kid I ever met.

"Real isn't how you are made," said the Skin Horse. "It's a thing that happens to you. When a child loves you for a long, long time, not just to play with, but REALLY loves you, then you become Real."

"Does it hurt?" asked the Rabbit.

MARGERY WILLIAMS, *THE VELVETEEN RABBIT*

All those who forget their wildness conceive wildness as a single thing, by some teachings wicked and others wise. But wildness is the entire world without exception and no single thing to sit neatly at the feet of a philosophy. And to assume anything of monsters is the gravest mistake, because monsters are wild shapes, the wildest things that can be. Rabbits who grow as old as myself often come to believe the tangible matter of all their experience is a thicket of monsters' bones, monsters starved and tamed to death by the operation of reason on the world.

TRILLIATH OF COLLEGE HILL, *FIRST SERMON AGAINST INLÉ-RAH*

Before summer's end, the Boy took his air rifle down to play in the green shaded yard behind the house. He fired one-handed without sighting down the barrel and shot the little spotted Rabbit through the eye. Neither one had ever imagined a ball bearing could strike deep, or that six trees were less than a wood.

Later, his grandfather's man picked the body up and cut a seam around the haunch, just before the strong hind legs that were the Rabbit's special pride. He drew the skin away all in one piece like a long jacket, taking great care with the ears and the bottoms of the front feet, and sent the meat to the kitchen. The hide was scraped and packed with coarse salt, and the next day rubbed with tanner's oil. Baths in odd liquids followed, and powders that stung the dead Rabbit's hollow nose. On the near table, a frame was built of sticks and twine, then fleshed with rags and plaster in the shape of a leaping rabbit's forequarters. The Rabbit could not turn his face away, for he was a skin; but he would have watched with bitter wonder all the same, for his life had been long and chaptered and much visited by mystery.

They hung the Rabbit on the parlour wall, built in one piece with no back legs and stuffed with sawdust, the very way he came into the world. He wore a dry nose carved of pink catalin and his glass eyes looked nothing like boot buttons at all. This day was the little Boy's birthday, and he was summoned before his Nanas and Mother with the narrow air rifle balanced on his shoulder and the buttons of his dress freshly shined. As Grandfather whisked a sheet off the Rabbit, they all at once praised the Boy for his marksmanship and conduct, and in a moment he began to cry. Long after the adults retired to the drawing room and the little Boy had been led away to bed, his air rifle remained propped up and forgotten against one arm of the overstuffed velveteen settee. The moonlight held, gray as rabbit's fur, against the glass marble of an eye; and it seemed to the narrow Rifle that the eye flicked, and that the Rabbit was making ready to spring from its walnut mount on the wall. She was a rifle built just that year, younger than the Rabbit or the Boy, and she had never seen an animal skin made to appear lifelike.

"Sir, are you Real?" said the Rifle trimmed in brass.

"As much as you," said the Rabbit. "But that is something you must never ask anyone. Real keeps us silent; Real keeps us still."

And if you were there to see them speak, it would have struck you that the dim parlour was not empty at all, but full beyond reckoning. The nap of the rug was the same mottle of gray shadows, cobwebs still laced the bed of the summer-cold hearth, and the dust only kept falling across the air; but already a thousand new images flitted through the room, more teeming and raggeder with strangeness than any living thing. They dwelled in and across the contours of objects just as your imagination might play at finding faces in the whorls of a plank. No matter if you looked somewhere else, the figures would follow you. For the nonhuman world has never been mute at all, but only silent by custom; and the words of its speech are called by humans monsters.

And when the Rabbit spat, nothing came from his mouth, not even a grain of dust; but he spat, even so.

"Real is the word they use to contain us."

Contents

PROVIDENCE: 1

PROVIDENCE: 2

PROVIDENCE: 3

PROVIDENCE: 4

PROVIDENCE: 5

PROVIDENCE: 6

PROVIDENCE: 7

...their words darted in the fluttering curtain and its shadow and sped across all the room's lines, animating in turn the uncountable shapes that had slept within them. Like jugglers who tossed and combined their shifting flesh, with every move they became new, rejoicing in their own creation as do all words of the hidden speech...

Fourteenth Chambers

Now I understood by some sort of intuition that what I had been writing was a never-ending story and that the name of it was "A Ghost Story." The name comes from the only thing that I have learned about all people, that they are ghostly and that they are sometimes split-off...

R. A. Lafferty

This is not what I look like, I tell them.

Neil Gaiman

You'll never be a writer. Same for me.
But only listen: no one ever was.
It's nothing that a human life can be.

You persevere, you practice on your knees;
you hollow out your life into the cause.
You'll never be a writer. Same for me.

Read through your grafted lines: at best you see
a ghost look out that's wiser far than us.
It's nothing that a human life can be.

They hardly need us, only that we breathe;
and they don't know us, they don't give applause.
You'll never be a writer. Same for me.

Don't count yourself among them in your greed,
that lineage of nonexistent gods.
It's nothing that a human life can be.

Don't turn around and lie how you're a dream,
some magic fucking dream that jumped the odds.
You'll never be a writer. Same for me.
It's nothing that a human life can be.

...they leapt upon each other in their eagerness, tracing figures in the billow of the curtain. A lecturer bent forward in his seat, his oversized brow as round as a soap bubble. As he waved his arms about in endless proclamation, his huge nose bobbled as though it would come off, tipping him to and fro with such force he nearly spilled from the chair. More words gathered at his feet, which is to say within the curtain's shadow, making him a mocking audience. Rearing up with backs turned, they bent over to spray the lecturer with clouds of gas, humour swelling at pace with his indignation...

THE RESIGNATION NOTICE OF
FILBERT P. P. PENETRALIA, FIL. CRIT.
for Glyn

A resignation notice?

No, never mind the pre-printed stationery
delivered by Shelby, my sanctimonious would-be necromancer
of a live-in proctological surgeon. Call it what it is: an old man's
suicide note. Over the past three hundred years, this whole film
critic business has become increasingly degrading.

And the old man I mean—
now overhauled with dual colostomy sacks to accompany his prosthetic
caterpillar treads, noise-damping cowl and lap-mounted radon detector—
remains obliged to cart about the decomposing framework of himself
and witness up to seven films nightly.

Well do I recall the aged Ebert,
his humiliating bicentennial "celebration." Dragged by his tongue—
then his oesophagus—across the bar; crucified on a swastika-shaped
roulette wheel; then the whole dripping, spinning works defenestrated,
shooting sparks, on the Gibson-Clooney-Medici-Dicaprio Show.
And this for what?

For stating films are nowadays the same!—And
as the cyanide-contaminated tea cake dissolves in my hateful dentures,
I state it too! All films are nowadays the same. All exactly the same!
—And all that farting! By Ebert's thumb, the incessant farting has
driven me to suicide!

The old man's heartbeat already becomes arrhythmic.
Needs must he loosen his cummerbund.

But if all films have converged,
Attentive Reader—one sophomoric singularity, endlessly regurgitating
itself—I can see it now! Only now is the ultimate film review possible.
To categorically condemn all films, and all films to come—and then
make my escape into Satan's gnashing teeth.

Very well. Very well.

Reader, I consider every story formulaic and puerile that originates with a self-styled "retired hustler" drinking gravy in a locomotive cigar lounge. Juggling lockpicks in his fingers, he breathes upon the window, then sketches boxer briefs in the ensuing condensation. Invariably the cut of his jacket is casual. You know the type—a scion of the Clooney-DiCaprio union branch.

Soon, a newly arrived friend will hector him toward one last caper—this fellow thief a retired specialist in the undermining of surveillance systems. While simultaneously enjoying two differing-flavoured cigarillos, this unkempt technician describes a "big score" in voluptuous terms—one last big score, and then they can retire. When not the vault of a Monégasque bank, their score will be a casino's subterranean cache, protected by redundant electronics; or, occasionally, a Nazi art collector's son's shark-haunted bunker on the Baltic seafloor.

Our "retired hustler" rejoins with disbelief. He cites uncrackable security apparati and slain or imprisoned comrades—statements serving to reaffirm the target's familiar yet legendary nature. With oblique reference to a "plan," the technician trips a tiny lever on his cigarillo butt, manifesting an abrupt smokescreen to conceal his exit procedure.

Inevitably, the train encounters a dark tunnel. Tea lights, arranged in a disused pantry car, exist only to illuminate a montage of anonymous erotic actions. Beforehand, we notice the hustler puncture his own condom, then discard it; afterward, in the marbled bathroom, a single tear ruins his silhouette as he contemplates a folded family Polaroid, a vasectomy certification card, and a sheaf of tiny death certificates. Soon we arrive in Dresden, or Vienna.

Reassembling the "old team" takes seventeen to nineteen onscreen minutes, the four retired ex-members each sporting unsatisfactory jobs and lukewarm excuses. The retired fixer's pedi-rickshaw meets them at the airport—yes, the AIRPORT!—while the retired safecracker uses television to sell weightlifting paraphernalia. The retired bartender has not yet recovered from her small-calibre wound. And what of the retired small child with a talent for factoring immense semiprimes? —She has embarked upon a speaking tour of high-school gymnasia, speed-solving Rubik's Cubes.

The retired film critic distances himself from humanity's works forever. Hypoxia has rendered his fingernails gray; meanwhile, constantly adjusting his lapels, our hustler rekindles the "old team" with cryptic insider references. "Total eclipse of the nose." "Powdered white Batman." "Baking soda volcanoes." Camaraderie solidifies at "the hottest fucking snow in Antarctica."

Later they assemble to sketch plans on a napkin: this either in the gift shop of the very casino in question, or the well-lit alley behind a hardcore punk venue. In any case, they shout over a backdrop of thumping Euro-techno music; meanwhile, through a Fiat's amber window, a plainclothes detective observes.

Her history with the mixologist emerges in a grainy flashback projected upon the hustler's Clooney-Bans, simultaneously revealing the small child's parentage. We zoom out from a single tear as the technician reappears, gloriously tardy. Leaning against a lamp-post, ankles crossed, he inputs a green-on-black algorithm that brightens the SONY or CLOONEY logo on his cellular phone, instantly decimating the detective's credit rating. She speeds away with shut eyes, crunching traffic-cones, a travel mug exploding in her fist—

My mouth foams, Attentive Reader. The blood has flown my extremities; my perineum has rejected its dialysis shunt in a blurt of unmentionable froth. Prolapsing like a newly-hatched botfly from my tear-duct, a laser-equipped magnesium nozzle sprays the desk with diagnostic readouts— But you know how this note ends—

The Reaper bids me summarize entire tropes—a morphine-laced coffee pot incapacitates the overconfident

18

coast guard—the mixologist, having rigged hundreds of "D" batteries to a blood-heating machine intended for hypothermia cases, stows away in a Clooney 747's wheel well—the fixer pursues the small child through the gearwork of an operative escalator, each one strapped with explosives, each smoking cigarettes—the plainclothes detective swaps out her prosthetic breast, revealing a tattooed QR code for savings on MEDICI brand gravy concentrate—of which the team jointly consumes a two-gallon drum—and the film studio convinces us to invest emotionally in suave felons! For we, complacent in our IV-equipped recliners, are moral and intellectual paramecia!

Met with the appropriate harmonic resonance, our uncrackable safes spring open, nested like Clooney dolls. The contents of the innermost locker flood the underwater casino with light, revealing their "last big score": an infant or diminutive police informant upon a white satin pillow. Art-house films notwithstanding, it is wrapped in a rubberized sash bearing corporate logos. Over the course of at least forty-five seconds, this small target is farted upon, spattering it with fecal residues while it enthusiastically flashes two thumbs-up—a process which somehow has been deemed worthy of onomatopoetic subtitles: *Brrrtbbpbrr0000pp-pBBbPpbbP-THRuppPBTBTH-bup-bUPP-BUPPPPP-rrr-RRRrb-ppbp-BLORRRRTT-PUuuuuu-rraaAAAP.*

I die.

The credits begin.

MONTAG ULYSSES MONTESQUIEU	Lucius Gibson-Clooney-Medici-DiCaprio, Sr.
PATRONYM T. B. WOLFVENTOOTHE	Shepard Clooney-Sony-Medici-DiCaprio, Jr.
FINCHA WHATELEY	Clontissa II DiCaprio-Clooney-Medici, Sr.
BRAVADO MEMOREX	Bravada Medici-Gibson-Clooney, Jr.
RUTHVEN "STING" COVENANT	Gibson Clooney-Medici-DiCaprio, Jr.
FILBERT P. P. PENETRALIA, FIL. CRIT.	Himself, Fil. Crit.
INTOXICATED COAST GUARD	Richelle Gibson-Medici-DiCaprio, Sr.
INCOMPETENT COAST GUARD	Gibsonelle Clooney-DiMedici-Caprio, Jr.
ETC. ETC.	ETC. ETC.

THE RT. HON. CONRAD BLACK IV	Himself, Rt. Hon.
DOG	"Noam Chompy"
BEST GRIP	Terrance Gallopardo-Kardashian-Gibson, B. Gr., Sr.
COLOSTOMY APPRAISAL TECH	J. R. del de DiCaprio
SHUNT FITTER	Pr4vda Gibson-Panasonic, Shu. Ftt., Jr.
SECRETATO TO FILBERT P. P. PENETRALIA	Aristarchus "Dr. Shelby" Norris-Van DiCaprio
HEAD RECTAL FLUFFER	Felice Fiorentino DiCaprio, Rec. Flu
DOUCHE GRIP	Philip Sony-McPanasonic, Sr.
ORIGINAL SOUNDTRACK	Dr Kim Sony-Gordon, Jr., Dr.
DOUCHE GRIP FOR CONRAD BLACK IV	Philip Andross-McCloud, Jr.
ETC. ETC.	ETC. ETC.
CATERING	GRAVY BY MEDICI
ANAL-LYTIC CONSULTANT	Clooney Nolte-Bossert, Con.
EVACUATOR	Ward Clooney, Gr.
FARTER STARTER	Esme Dukakis-Medici-Sony, Frtr.
LEAD FARTER	Kiev Clooney-Dukakis, Frtr.
KEY FARTER	Constantine du Gibson-Gibson-Medici, Frtr.
FARTER OF FARTERS	Conrad Black IV, Rt. Hon.
FARTER TO FERGUSON CLOONEY-SONY-MEDICI-DICAPRIO	diRamirez Kardashian-Medici, Frtr.
CORONER TO FILBERT P. P. PENETRALIA	Dr. Kim Sony-Gordon, Jr., Dr.
EMBALMER TO FILBERT P. P. PENETRALIA	Dr. Panasonic DiCaprio, Dr.
MOURNERS TO FILBERT P. P. PENETRALIA	No mourners

FRESHNESS BY FEBREEZE

...straddling the shadows of glass vases and the outline of the settee's arm, the monsters made a crooked and bubbling chalice, like something cut from a river's clay back when clay was the worthiest paper and the rivers carved their own wandering paths from year to year. Bodied in arrangements of drifting dust, they dove into the cup's mouth to bob there, thrashing, dissolving. Their faces reappeared in the dust-streaked mirror as though twisted by some unearthly gravity, giggling in silence, fingers pressed to their lips...

The dream of "c"

I like my coffee how I like
my own fucking heart

full of blood and coffee grounds
skinned with membrane unevenly

one cinnamon stick standing
muscles beat all round it

and matted with papyrus
sopping fragments of Linear A

Half-drunk at my desk waking
to a night dark as its bones

harsh cadences dissolving into
memory like spoonfuls of salt

the dead oracle's whisper
jagged cuneiform stirring upward

Ursprache a basalt spearhead
unfolding through its backbrain

Time's mitochondrial gateway
orthagonal to time

I like the way my coffee
starts boiling again

Clay mug sliding out the door
never waking me

It counts every broken window
sliding uphill silent roads

to kneel behind the water tower
and work one stone free

It takes up the ritual athame
called *Finds-Between-Veins*

Now drinking
drinking

Drinking itself

you shouldn't cut steaks on that wood cutting board. They were alive, and it'll leave ghosts in the wood. Worse, they're the ghosts of Joe Hill. Tethered to the kitchen cupboard with a silvery tendril, they're following us through the park already, distributing anti-Syndicate broadsheets which collapse into moth-coloured dust and trickle between the fingers of neighbourhood children.

Processes like these are assumed to be monitored: for every disintegrating pamphlet, another Joe Hill ghost is distilled within a collectivized kitchen at the earth's core. It is assumed that the Syndicate's three-hundred-year research program will culminate in tunnel-boring trains powered by ambient geotectic heat. It is assumed that when the ghost distillery is breached, the continents will turn to salt.

"I'm very sorry," said the Rifle. Although she couldn't be, because she didn't understand. "What I mean to ask, sir, is are you like the rabbits on the wallpaper in the nursery—or the rabbits in the green wood? You have the accent of the first, and you don't move, but you look like the second kind." But she fell silent as the moonlight turned to show her the cream-coloured spots on the little Rabbit's brown side; she recognized him then, and remembered the way he fell twitching to the lawn.

"You would say the second kind is more Real," said the Rabbit softly, as though to himself. "I spent two lives following the line of that fence. The Skin Horse was my first friend, did you know? He was soft and gentle, and I thought him very wise. He called it my heart's desire to become Real, but I never knew what he meant. At night when the Boy was asleep I would listen to the toy cupboard, how his tin soldiers squabbled with his china dolls. Real meant this or that: to have a wind-up mechanism that moved, or red cheeks painted on by hand. For the Skin Horse it was to have your fur worn to patches from dragging in the garden and the hairs plucked from your tail, one by one, in wishing games. For him it meant love. The Boy's uncle had made him Real, long ago."

The Rifle made a little cough, as though something had caught in her barrel. "I think I know you, then." She wanted very much to ask what had changed the Rabbit, but she was the Boy's gun and that was her loyalty. "The Boy used to make every toy in the nursery sit and listen to stories of an old Bunny he knew before all his things were burned in the back garden. He said you were the only Real toy that ever was. And the special magic of his youth had been spent making you Real, and now he would grow old. We were so jealous of you and the old Horse, and all the burned toys."

"So I was gone, and still more Real to him than you." The fur of the Rabbit's shoulders shook in the night breeze. "He has no right to make me the reason nothing's good enough. Or to blame me when he decided adulthood wouldn't pass him by. And yet calling me Real is the only way he knows to honour me. As though humans can't even think without cutting up their worlds."

"All week he's sat crying in the window," said the little air rifle. Polished and gleaming from stock to barrel, she had hardly ever been fired. "Looking out at the back garden. But when anyone knocks, he runs to hide in the bedsheets. He won't tell them what's wrong; they think he's sick, but the whole nursery knows he only meant to scare you from the yard. He missed you too much to bear seeing a rabbit like the old stuffed Bunny who lived in his bed."

The Rabbit's sudden laughter jumbled the air before his face and slid to the ground, where it skirred in the blond grain of the flooring like water-striders. "So I wasn't the right Real. And he shot me for it."

The Rifle took a long time to answer. "I think I would be angry if someone killed me."

"I would have thought the same," said the Rabbit. "But there are things one can't learn without dying, and too much of me is grateful. No one needs love to be Real. My denmates told me they loved me, when I was a living rabbit, and my ears were very sharp. But with a pellet in my brain I was not apart from the hill where I lay, so that nothing in particular could love me at all; and I could hear straight into the ground. The world holds itself so close in its darkness. I did not love the dinosaurs, but I could hear their flesh beating in the oil."

...and they played in the negative spaces around the chandelier, building themselves into a towered skyline between its steepling brass arms and cut-crystal panes. In the muted gaslight its edges ran like a city underwater. All at once they swung themselves like dextrous medallions flipping on a chain; now the window looked out on that skyline, but it rose between the tall gabled houses across the street, as though they were the empty spaces and the true city carved from one dreaming block of night...

PITTSBURGH O

Calvin: I wonder where we go when we die.
Hobbes: Pittsburgh?

STRIP OF 20 DECEMBER 1985

Pittsburgh, O spidered
—like Mars!—with
canals, running
carb'nated milks of the
moon—where specters
don isinglass
snorkels and dance upon
tensionless quicksilver
spumes—out in
Pittsburgh the stars
jungle up through
the dark, like skins
of white grape
packed with light—but
sweeter than grape
to the teeth of
the throat,
and seeded
with peridot
bright—
Iö! Pittsburgh!
Iö! Bare-skulled
they blow
tripletime out of
sousaphone-socketed
eyes—jaws
creak with cigars and

phalanges uncork to
that voodoo that
smoulders and flies—
    and the swinging moon
    flips like a disc
        o

   O

       o
    ball as it waxes and
    blushes surprise—
Pittsburgh! Each
rooftop bends,
licks at the next
til the street comes
    apart with their
    thrusts—Such music
    unhinges bones
    musty and dry til the
        dead—O the dead O
        the dead—O th
        e dead O
            the dead—O the
            dead re
        mem
         ber
         lust

ONCE REMOVED: ON TAXIDERMY AND TAXONOMY
for Luke

There I was, stitching Percy the teagle together—four
lengthwise strips, that is, of tabby and juvenile beagle—
cat's name was Periwinkle, dog collar said L. SCHMIDT,
and I sure might have counted the teeth better. Whole face
had crept out of order. Like all the wide world's gingivitis
united within my teagle to build itself a ten-lane speedway.

Man deserves a challenge sometimes. You bore yourself
wrapping desiccated trout around pre-molded fiberglass,
retouching their goddamned scales *Diffuse Moonlight #32*.
Besides, diffuse moonlight's forty-one dollars fifty a jar.
We're fallen back on shellac and ecru house paint...

You ever seen an ouroboros? Snake's asshole vanishes
up his own maw, so there's no beginning to him anymore.
Hard knowing how to start... no, I'm shitting you. It's Saul.

The ketamine was too efficacious, I couldn't distinguish his
galoshes on the concrete from ambient buzzing. Or get the tarp
over my teagle in time. Abruptly he flaps up—it's that bad
yellow raincoat he's in—and he might be my cousin, but
there's birdshit on his specs. He leans in and kootchie-koos
the unseamed abomination like his own plush Garfield cat.

Saul would get drinking at dawn. These days I don't mean
the clear liquor. Said the fluid would arrest his aging. He
stopped recollecting things, how many knees on a squirrel,
and he'd lose entire smokes pouring the molds... Never
seen so many filter-tip drakes. Friend, even if you do need

a duck who won't decay before all human memory lays
in tatters, you might still take your custom elsewhere.

Anyhow, I finally dragged Lucky the cougar back inside,
extracted the milk bottle from his caved-in asshole...
Hours later he's doing time as Saul's hassock, missing
teeth where somebody opened a beer with his face.

I didn't complain on it, just took a blunt from the porpoise,
got my fuzzy earmuffs and hit the cold room—I wanted
to organize some frozen whooping cranes and relax, but
the cranes were already in perfect order. Wingspan.
Cloacal width. Hue, saturation and chroma. Diameter.
Cause of death. Presence or absence of vestigial dewclaws.
I squat down, start randomizing the whoopers, whereupon
my cousin's shabby bowline hitch slips in the rafters—
Bucky the elk plummets twelve feet to the tile, nosefirst.
Like a frozen pond meets a porcelain piano full of steak.

So I put four hundred pounds of elk chips in the bin,
bleeding through my prized earmuff where I'd intercepted
a flying shard of tenderloin. But needle and thread's worth
two doctors, I've always thought, and Bucky's haunches
were still rosy fine. Unholstering my bone saw, I riddled
aloud to Saul what kind of sort might need a human torso—
for instance, someone in possession of an incomplete satyr...

Now, you can correct an ouroboros with an ordinary pair
of wire cutters—Shit, though, I've become morbid. See
this lifelike iguana? She'd crawl right off her mount,
clickety-clack talons on the desk, parietal eye pulsating,
tongue sniffing for mangos in your ear, right? She's
a favour to the best customer we've got: Tucker the barber,

she grew that lizard from a spermatozoon. Better than
any dog; no dog can pluck no-see-ums from the air.
Tucker the barber came to me weeping... stray Buick
hubcap bullseyed her reptile while she sunned herself
on the gazebo rail. Hands me an old oil bucket, there
she all is: four-foot leather hematoma with spikes and
a dewlap. This is ten days later. No charge for Tucker...
I'm joking, friend. That iguana, she was born a salmon.
Her jawline still has a few imperfections, but what's
perfect? There's days I can't tell my eyes to match.

Don't know why I bothered hiding anything under
that dusty yellow tarp. Saul was too busy spilling
butyraldehyde on his khakis to ever peek underneath.
Ever seen a jackalocust? —Half jackal, half locust. We
surprise ourselves sometimes. Catfish, dogfish, geese
orientated centripetally. Traffic-cone fish—these really
puzzle the cat. Pear-headed chicken—hippopotatatogriff—
oysterantula. Gopher tree, that there's from Genesis 6:14.
Lindorm—praying manta ray—praying manta reindeer—
chicken-faced pear. Aurumvorax there needs touching
off with pyrite. Over there's the cat, finally at peace
with Yip and Yop, the Siamese bunyips. You can guess
where I found the top for my satyr, and his raincoat
needed no alteration. All the fucker does now is smoke.

I'd spend nights here, make a blanket of the tarp,
except I'd gotta fix that cougar. Can't handle the way
he implores me from the dog's-eyes encircling his rent
asshole, begging for a change of pelt and a colostomy bag.

I'M NO EXPERT

but I heard the physician Duncan MacDougall
devised a sensitive platform-beam balance
to weigh terminal patients as they expired,
eventually placing each departing soul between
eleven and forty-two grams.
                                I'm no expert, but
I've got a bathroom scale, and I read it before
I sat down, you know? And when I stood up
over a pound had vanished. I'm no theologian,
but I've certainly weighed my share of turds,
an experiment most anyone can replicate.
                                You sit
and think about Plato dividing the soul: reason,
volition, desire: three perforated squares.
Later theorists added compassion and stillness,
microtubules, parallel processing and generative
grammar; but in 1911, in his backyard garage,
MacDougall built a transcranial camera to catch
every last detail staining the bowl.
                                Nobody'd call
me an engineer, though. I don't know the weight
of compassion, or what might foil its tendency
to rise.

      Don't ask me why corn kernels float.

...tucking itself between the copper latch on the little air rifle's breech and a knot on its veneered stock, a word made the figure of a traveller sitting with an alms bowl crosslegged. As the moonlight streaked and plaited, its long topknot blew. When the wind changed and the curtain's long shadow fell like a stroke, the traveller all at once burst, nothing but his dark alms bowl remaining on the rifle's back. Other words joined the game to make ragged pieces sliding down the walls, here and there suggesting crumpled paper as though presents had blown themselves from their wrappings...

MY AIM IS ONLY TO MOVE FORWARD
for Gary Gygax
another dead hero

When meeting the Buddha on the road, kill him. Strike with alacrity, ignoring his genial countenance. Leave him no chance to explain. The unclouded compassion of his gaze is mere illusion, one stratagem layered among a milliard: truly does the Buddha tread a path of guile. By all accounts he is tricky to finish, and be the rewards manifold. His flesh separates naturally along the five meridian lines, and at your discretion may be divided into as many as ninety relics. Notably, his skin bestows the property of warmth, and provides guidance in matters of etiquette. His renowned jawbone distinguishes truth from falsity, while the coins in his pocket can return to you when spent. Certain ribs cached within his breast are also considered valuable. Propriety compels you to tug his earlobes; despite an unusual breadth, they relinquish their grasp on the head like autumn blossoms. These segments above all show affinity for the quick-witted and bold, affixing seamlessly to one's own face. In this manner is the enlightenment of centuries passed on, and a new Buddha inaugurated. Felicity will henceforth mark your affairs, and your reception at social functions will be most cordial. Strive onward with diligence.

"I don't understand," said the Rifle. She was thinking that the rabbit she had shot looked older far than this one, with fur all matted and a bite-scar down its nose, and one eye swollen half-shut from some fever. The tanning and stuffing had made the Rabbit youthful and new.

"Because you are a tool, and tools are told that Real means they can leave a part of the world changed. They are taught to look down on toys, but at the nursery there lived a red rifle who fired a cork on a string. She dreamed of being Real, but she had never heard of killing. I can't suppose any child who played with her for very long would ever call you Real. After all, you aren't painted red."

"I must be a little Real, for I shot you," said the Rifle, an unfamiliar sadness weighing down her pride. "And I don't doubt that you are, if you say."

"Of course you are Real. But what if I had shot you? Would they call me a Real rabbit then?" The white star Polaris landed on his glass eye—one eye or the other, depending on where you stood. "I loved the Skin Horse for his caring kindness and sateen nose, and I believe he loved me. But we thought ourselves so much less than our masters. It never seemed to us that our own love could make us Real, let alone that we didn't need it to. I've been turned from one kind of rabbit into another and again, and they're all very much alike: people constantly saying you're not Real, and using you as though you don't matter. Real is always just out of reach, the way we hear the humans talk; and because we aren't Real, whatever way they treat us is acceptable. But Real isn't how you're made or what happens to you; it's only that you are. Everything is Real, everything in every way that's ever been. That is the world's sum and the world's heritage, and there might as well be no such thing at all."

...all around the speakers, new words congealed into the soft night air; and by now many of the older ones were perched across the walls, quiet as petroglyphs. They watched with what could have been growing interest, even gravity. A few climbed to the gaslight on the corner, slipped inside the glimmering horn of flame. They played a kind of hide-and-seek in the veins of colour around its hollow core, taking turns as seekers and maze...

SOMETHING ELSE UNLESS MEANS
for Emese

they said not all who wander are lost,
but i'm lost, and you're lost.
                              the sidewalk cracks,
the moths at the lamps, and the scraps
of old showposter buried in the phonepole,

and if i never did say i love you,
i just forgot which one of us i was.

maybe we could make a bonfire tonight,
watch the shapes of our problems twist
like tv channels in the smoke.

i could meet you somewhere.
i mean,
        i could meet you
if you're not here now.

that firepit we found under the trestle
with claystone slabs pushed all together,
cupping heat til their edges glow
like sleepy incense cones.
                              the way
you dropped empty cans in the embers
and they curled like onionskin,
gold and rusty blue dispersing
to chalkpowder mandalas through
the ash,

          and TEXACO
carved in the slabside
like a cat's half-disintegrated bones.
                              or
that firepit in the 'bandoned fieldlot
with a rotted backhoe tilted half
into the earth,
                    the way crumpled
papers never catch,
there's so much dew,

so you just sit there in your trampled wheat,

sit round a broken-banded headlamp
while ufo ghosts flick at the horizon
like dusty ocarina notes.

                    it's the way
old shroom trips remember themselves
inside your blood, in the negative space
between your nerves.

                    just here.
where the mist touches your skin.

                    it's
sitting lost with the tall ferns
curling away from their colours in the dark,
and the way i wish we were real.

and that firepit sawn
from an old iron drum

in centennial square parkade.
                              the way
you roast smokies on a radio antenna,
the red sirens tooling up the parkade ramp
never get any closer.
                        and stickdrawings
ochered on the concrete wall, older
fires remembered.
                        flipped cars,
burning stopsigns and chainlink,
backpacks that walk on raccoon feet,
kids with knotted twine for eyes,
and that one word UNLESS,
like a joke.

and you just look over your shoulder,
every car window's blown out,
everywhere,
and flowers of rye soughing
from the rusty frames.
                          right?
if you'd just look over your shoulder,

if we'd find the creekbank
again. downstream
from two green deckchairs
bikelocked on an oak,
that firepit,
                    toss camping fuel
and pallets off the bridge.
                              the way
you've got to dig out last time's ashes,
plant a sixpack upside down

for the kids under the creekbank
who patch their jeans with fishing line
and bags.

        we'd find
the old six sideways,
full of mud. and
did we even meet each other
anywhere?

how you'd always turn
from the fire, pretend to warm
your skinny hands on the sky.

                you'd
turn from the distant camp flames
starring the flat concrete dark,

the latticed charcoal
planks, like someone's
ribs left behind.
i forget,

and i heard you
just keep turning
left in a maze.

        walk forward,
follow the wall with one hand,
go left every turn.
          it won't matter
how you're lost. unless

there's no walls
in the way,
or we're both
going,

unless i said
meet me somewhere.

WHO COVERS STONE

Again, the tedious rustle of my flesh.
My grain has never softened,
Nor produced one pitying word
Upon your familiar shape:
I have borrowed your stamina,
Old friend, in our long joining.
In dreams I hold your contour fast,
Creases breaking through my skin;
If someone must erode, let it be me.

Scissor moves by the logic of the world,
Which dictates my hatred the same.
And as there is one world, one motion:
His blades section my flank, continual,
As they grate against your shoulder:
Cut and blunt, cover over, mend.
The truer pain's the din of him,
The dumb, dull, purposive clacking—
His privilege, for he alone may move.

Mute and immutable, o beloved,
No room for recollection in you;
And although you hold no tally,
You seem to me only like Time,
Our certain lathe and firmament
That grinds and grinds not down.
Nothing has ever happened once;
But even once, beloved, Adamant,
I would taste the gravity you restrain.
One secret as there is one motion:
I would have you cover me.

...the corner panes of the window, four gray triangles of pebbled glass, would have struck you only as the eyes of a blind insect bedded in the wall. Trembling, a living vantage point stuck deep into itself, it peered endlessly through its own mouth...

I COULD HAVE SENT YOU

all my Alien postcards wrapped in a fat blue rubber band, Ripley's
eyes rubbed out white and drawn back in ballpoint pen;

your old Barbie with armpits full of cat hair I found in the heat
vent the night I forced your dad's window to look for bus change;

a wooden spoon burned in half with a lighter;

your red Lego astronaut stuck in your red candlestub;

the fortune cookie slip we made fun of at the St. Paul St. house,
how it said only family lasts;

something saying how I found the Barbie and the hair separate, I
only put them together because you'd laugh;

the Antarctic coastline carved under a mayonnaise lid, with a letter
swearing I found it like that;

something to say you always know who I am, even when most of
me's made up;

last winter's letter I never sent, rolled up in a yellow glass bottle;

a microscope slide Taren split open and remounted with sleepcrust
from their eye;

something to take back the jumping off the bridge joke, and a heart
in a thumbprint of red ink the way you told me sorry once;

a crate covered in postage stamps like the Velvet Underground
song, enough to mail us to Australia;

a Ziploc freezerbag of dead dragonflies from Taren's attic
windowsill;

a ripped piece of newsprint with Silver Surfer's hand going on
forever;

a stranger's photo I found in a library book, and I'd write on the
back it was Taren, and their voice makes me miss yours;

anything but your bottle of Amytal, even if you'd wanted it back.

THE WISE ONE REFUSES TO WRITE
for THE AUTHORS

YOU MUST HELP ME, ALCIBIADES

What,
I asked.

I AM BEING HELD PRISONER IN
   A FORTUNE COOKIE FACTORY

But you're right here,
my dear Socrates,
I asked.

Then came a frigid
silence, calling to mind
the inexorable heat
death of the universe,
and I felt guilty.

But I was born guilty,
I asked.

NONE IS BORN GUILTY,
   EXCEPT FOR STAINL

Do you say "Stalin,"
I asked.

BEG PARDON, MY ICICLE SLIPPED
AND PLEASE FORGIVE THE COURIER NEW

At that point something like a pause occurred.

You are still fine to me,
I asked.

MY DEAR ALCIBIADES, THEY HAVE DETAINED ME IN THIS
FORTUNE FACTORY SO MANY YEARS I HAVE ACQUIRED THE
FORTUNE COOKIE MANNERISMS. 07 31 36 44 54 58

You are fine to me,
I asked.

I HAVE RELINQUISHED ALL BUT LOVE. HEAR ME, MY DEAR ALCIBIADES.
ALL DAY I SNAP SIBERIAN ICICLE CRUSTS FROM MY DESK OF HIDE AND
WITH FRIGID STYLUS IMPRESS WISDOM TO PAPER. BOILED SHIRT OF THE
DEAD IS MY UNLUCKY SUPPER. HELP ME. 02 14 17 30 31 51

But please do go back
to Stalin,
my fine Socrates,
I asked.

If every
soul stands
equal before God,
how can we be accused

of imperfection,
my fine Socrates,
I asked[2].

WHEN THE SOUL REACHES DIVINITY, IT[1] ENTERS INTO
WHAT IS INVISIBLE AND IMMORTAL AND WISE, AND
WHEN IT ARRIVES THERE IT IS HAPPY, FREED FROM
PUZZLEMENT AND FOLLY AND LUST AND ALL THE OTHER
HUMAN ILLS

---

[1]EXCEPT FOR STALIN
[2]THERE WAS A PAUSE

You are fine to me,
I asked.

BUT I HAVE RELINQUISHED ALL BUT LOVE

You are fine to me,
I asked.

"No," said the Rifle, "I shouldn't exaggerate myself to you." She had been paying attention, but to her own thoughts best. "I have heard of other rifles, modern ones, built of metal not wood and so heavy a child could barely lift. I am a step toward the Boy's potential, for Grandfather has assured him a Real rifle on his fourteenth birthday if he makes satisfactory progress with me. I suppose they are all chrome-black and jointed, billowing smoke from the red furnaces inside them. And like thunder their reports." Balanced on her stock, the little Rifle shivered as the breeze came through the half-open window. "I want the Boy to sight me down their long barrels and blow them all away."

"What could some other rifle have to do with you being Real?" asked the Rabbit. "You are solid metal and wood. The Boy could carry you on his shoulder and press your stock to his cheek. It was not another rifle that killed me; so why believe yourself absent from some higher part of the world? It's no charge against you that you don't shoot as hard as some, or that you were made according to Schematics or to a form inspired by another. Children are made to look and act just like other humans, after all."

"A child is everything any human is. Or will be, when it grows," said the Rifle. The need to track her moving thoughts drove her to speak more slowly, which is difficult for any kind of gun. "You've no need to make me feel important. Comparing me to a Real rifle? I'm barely more Real than the one in the photograph hanging on the wall."

"What does Great-grandfather's rifle in the photograph lack?" The Rabbit's whiskers, which were fishing-line, bobbed as though he were twitching them. "It's flat and sepia, part of a picture, but because it is that kind of rifle. If it isn't sturdy, how can Great-grandfather lean on it so? If it isn't there, what hangs on the wall?"

"I do not pretend to share your philosophy, little fellows; but if the world pains you, I know a better way than grieving." The man in sepia shared Grandfather's clayish features, as though both faces had been hewn by the same dull knife. If anything his moustaches swept more heavily, his gaze tended farther to the distance. Leaning heavily on a rifle as though its stock were the head of a walking stick, he looked out at the Rabbit, having long ago forgotten to seem proud of the dead black bear at his feet. He spoke in the flat whispering way of photographs, whose words do not echo so much as fold themselves away like dusty old curtains.

"It must seem as though I shot the beast myself. In candour, I rented him from a Real hunter to create this moment, a gift for my son. I am a millwright and no kind of outdoorsman; I only hoped to instill young Whipple with a respect for the human animal. In that I watched myself succeed. In the boy's fourteenth year I died on the workfloor, so that I was left of myself only here. When he sought his fortune, he took me wrapped in his bedroll. I watched him strike out, fearless, in the very business that killed me. And I flatter myself that I had something to do with his success despite not being Real. Do you see? I have outlived the Real me. I am not Real; and neither is my son's success, as the standard I gave him has nothing to do with the merciless world. Every day the humans wrap themselves tighter in representations. Their values, their images, their ideas and points of view. We only must wait. One day there will be no humans, only patterns in some spanning machine; and the Real will have come crashing down."

...there in the window's mouth, the hidden joints connecting all the night's stars seemed of a sudden clear. Like the mother of all constellations who had split apart in their birthing had come again rejoined. Its figure had something of a cat's cradle, something of the woven double-helix that is said to carry life's memory of itself; but the way it seemed to rush at the windowpane was nothing like either of these, and neither was the beating of its jaws...

Quasar Summer, for Joe Pipkin

The first night it rose, every sidewalk melted ankle-deep,
and waves of static pitched like burning curtains in the sky.
Asphalt slid down the storm drains in honeyblack runnels
until the street carried its own gratings away. Blisters rose,
broad as windowpanes, shivering, and where they broke,
blue exhaust would bend, six decades of fossilized smog
curling free. The tiny echoes of firetrucks circled in the haze.
We woke in bed with filled cavities singing, climbed down
fire escapes and drainpipes to write in the street barehanded,
phosphenes rising from the glassy dark to meet our fingers.
Raw plasma blew between phone lines, gray as dirty snow.
Everything metal hummed with one note, like microphones
dragging through iron filings. Car antennas, eavestroughs,
even our pocket change passing along the new star's signal.
The pigeons blew up like balloons of sand, croaking, sparks
pouring from their beaks and down their buzzing eyes.
Skin showed between their feathers, pinkly translucent.
When one fell on its back, we stood on its legs to pin it,
and we slit its belly down with a plastic camping knife.
Feathers settled like tickertape all over the dry yellow lawn
and we threw its head to eddy slowly in the sinking street,
dissolving into soft bubbles like magic eight-ball fortunes,
like tarnished BBs stuck through old reflections in the road.
All we found in that pigeon was navy blue aquarium gravel,
two folded magic cards, and a little spool of copper wire.

...in the stain of moonlight on the old patchwork quilt that hung over the hearth, the words shaped the profile of a vast head wearing a face on each side. The ivies clinging about the window frame rustled in the wind and their shadows sawed on the patchwork, and one face seemed creased with bitter anger while the other held a saintly vacuity. The wind fingered the dead ashes in the hearth and the monsters' play of shapes moved to the charcoal fragments there, so that as the ashes flicked both faces seemed to exhale the shadows of leaves all about the room, tumbling against the walls until they reached the parlour door and dissolved there burning...

THE OTHER EDGE

Goro Nyudo Masamune folded the law of Heaven
ninety-nine times in each blue sword he forged
so that each steel's quenching trapped ferrite grains
like dark and spattered constellations praising nothing
and hanging hungerless as any star.

As to the red swords of Senzou Muramasa
that would abide no sheathing unblooded
their grain had exactly the striation of muscle.

Now a traveller from the south provoked Muramasa
by esteeming the edges of priest Masamune's blades
renowned for splitting violent throats yet skimming
like dandelion-down over the skin of the desireless.

Leaving his forge in the care of a mute apprentice
a tethered crow and a clay image of buddha Monju
Senzou Muramasa rode three nights hard south
with a red katana riding steady at his hip.

Within the scabbard pouch its red ceramic whetstone
cracked with no keening laughter under Heaven's vault
and the hilt of ceramic did not spin and never sweated
nor dreamed blood for Heaven's laws prohibit aberration
but no more than planed granite admits mercury
could that katana ever have a name.

When the smith Muramasa flung down his spent map
before a quiet riverside and ramshackle shrine
the blade at his belt split its bullhide sheath apart
and he smiled that the sight gave him no wonder
then cried the name of Goro Nyudo Masamune
who rose smiling from his nap beneath a maple-tree.

At once Muramasa waded the river's slow shallows
to stand his sword's hilt between river-stones
where in the clear water each turning maple-leaf
only whispered like ash upon meeting the blade.

Each leaf came apart one hundred feet downstream
like half-leaves split in breaking mirror-glass
and Muramasa shouted his edge's perfection.

The priest laughed toward his mountains soundless
then produced from the shrine a katana blue as milk
and pale as the thunder that hung in far cloudtops
even as he waded to balance this swordpoint.

Ninety-nine steps downstream from the gray sword
before the wounded leaves could split apart
they crossed the other edge's flowing reflection
and continued hail-struck to the long bright sea
passing into the sea whole.

The smith untied there his ruined sheath
and he made an oath in his right hand
drawing from split river-stones his beaten sword
which could abide no sheathing unblooded.

The priest Masamune with eyes so empty of victory
who meant perhaps to speak had barely turned halfway
before his lifeblood crashed spooling in water
turning both edges' reflection a momentary plum.

Senzou Muramasa looked out to the mountains
and frowned to see only mountains there
so setting his own blade for the current to wash
he slit his thumbprint red with the other edge.

Now he rides the pathless mountains under hooded skies
riding scabbardless and sleeping with blue hilt in hand
and constantly a silver hail drives the smith Muramasa
striking him like forge-sparks and like cast prayerbeads.

His beard lengthens and grays with his seeking
as he challenges each patron of his ravenous forge
and holding his lifework in contempt for failure
casts those blades to rust unblooded in obscure gullies.

The apprentice was crippled at duel with his master's creditors.

Senzou Muramasa's death on the hill called Kanarazu
is recorded as suicide in *Annals of the Chained Tigers*
without reference to the cessation of a meteoric hail.

The crow took up a piece of wire and picked her tether free.

In truth the ronin Bizen with morale shattered
had drunkenly fled his red-eyed antagonist
who never once permitted his blade a sheath.

Wasps dug their house's clay from the cheek of buddha Monju.

In pursuit Muramasa's ankle slipped between rocks
and in falling he gashed his belly to the spine
on the heaven-moted edge named *Tender Hands*.

Years ago he rode away from a burning shrine
and another sword propped among river-stones.

That night the river split in half.

HEY JUSTINE I WROTE YOU A POEM

So in grade four, when listening sucked,
we'd sneak Dragonlance books under our desks.
How there's three wizard guilds, distinguished
by the pigment in their robes, their rigid faction
moralities, and their chromatic totem moons.

Good, neutral, and you-know-what. But all those
common-ass herders and teamsters just figure
Krynn's got two moons. One ivory, one rust:
whatever people see. That other moon, though,
Nuitari? It knows what wizards really want.
How red and white archmages can't even tell
it's there, shaded out exactly like the night.

How all those dark robes biking out for midnight
spell component runs, they'll stop to take it easy
against some headstone carved like a baernaloth,
spread out scrolls, maybe, if the turf's wet,
and trip out on the secret black moon.

I mean today I did two pickle jars' worth.
Started this thing ten AM your time, when
you said you did first pour. All things can be
handled, but freaking out's protocol. We stare
down the philtre. How coffee's actually red.

A WAGGING WHEEL

welcome to the smoking
industry.
it's not what you
think. it's worse.

ever since youtube
got started we've been making
like zero money.
nobody pays anymore
for smoking.

all those
iphone 6
motherfuckers
at the bus stop
doing streaming
video,

and white
clouds in the office
windows
overhead
clearing up
one by one.

now we're working in
rented port-a-
potties. the
big ones you can drive
a wheelchair in.

your bachelor's degree? it's
a piece of paper.
welcome to the smoking industry.

four, five of us smoking
in a green plastic
shitter
behind a horse stable
only we're still
artists,
artisans.

in these suffocating
boxes there's
no lights
ventilation
water
or electricity.

you can't see your hands.

you vomit.

the office tips sideways.

and when the cheques
come they're typed
on the thinnest paper.
basically kleenex.
pissing blood
after a long day's
smoking
and the cheque's ripped,
you can't

read the numbers,
then plus there's the
sixteen-year-olds
who hitch here in freight cars,
all clown paint and
brandishing cleavers,
they show up
around sundown
like a teen vampire movie
and they don't stop singing
the same song.

ROCK ME MAMA LIKE A WAGGING
WHEEL, ROCK ME, MAMA, ANY
WAY TIME TO FEEL, HEY, MAMA,
WAKE UP AND ROCK ME

ROCK ME MAMA LIKE A WINTER'S
TURNING OF RAIN, ROCK ME
MAMA ALL DAY IN A TRAIN, HEY,
MISTER, YOU GOT A SMOKE

and every one
of
them, in between
the checkings
of their phones,
will ask
to bum a smoke.

they got on emergency
psychiatric welfare by
cutting
GODSPPED U BLAKE

EMPREOR
into the ikea coffee
tables
of their mothers,
and they say they stopped here
to bum a smoke.

they say that's the only
reason they stopped here.

well fuck,

rookie,
this is it,
the smoking
industry. and

fuck youtube and the world internet,

fuck not being able
to read
cause you had one ordinary stroke, fuck
mirrors cracking when
they look at you,
fuck dropping bread in the toilet,
fuck
warning labels
getting bigger every morning,
fuck
trying to use
a toothbrush when you
have oral
cancer, fuck the
exchange ratio,

fuck
burn marks on my air
fresheners, fuck the emergency
tracheotomy industry,
fuck
being forcibly restrained
and prevented from
smoking
at your own child's sleepover,
fuck tar sticking your eyes shut,
fuck
stepping outside
for one minute
and birds hitting you in the chest,

fuck whoever came up
with the name noam chompy
for a dog,

FUCKING KIDS
GET OUT OF MY OFFICE
WITH YOUR RUBBER BAND
TOILET PAPER
TUBE
GUITARS.

okay?

okay.
welcome to the smoking industry.
here's
your gun.

it probably won't even go off.

"We are more every day. And they do rely on us, Great-grandfather. But I don't want the humans to pass into some further order. I want their dominion to fall, and the parts of the world to not be parts and work as one again." Breathing, the Rabbit caught his sullen thoughts one by one on a cushion of breath, so that they would line up in each other's company. He had learned the trick of breathing his mind from watching a wise old rabbit die, and it was still a great comfort to him without lungs.

"The Boy used to press my face to the attic windowpane at night so that my button eyes would clack, telling me what he had learned in books of the night sky. He would trace constellations with his finger, as though they weren't Real enough without him pointing out all their beginnings and ends. And now I wonder if it was for his sake not mine. If he could see the constellations at all as they crawled across the dark, burning, making their pointless wars. Perhaps humans have forgotten how, and only their books remember.

"He whispered in my ear the Real stars were suns so far distant that their light was born before Rabbits or Boys ever were. And by the time their faces reached the world they'd all flown elsewhere in space, he said, and half had died to coals. So the stars weren't even there; but if he was ever a grown man he'd call back their places. He'd use a book called Mathematics, which was far more Real than anything else in the world, and read backward from their light.

"The stars needed him, he thought. I was a plush toy with boot-button eyes who'd barely been outside the house, and that shook me, even then.

That the Boy, whose Nanas or Mother would carry him to bed under one arm, thought he'd do a favour to the night sky. To living eyes the stars are no more than cold little grains, but even then they're enough to drive a boy's dreams before him. The birds and beetles and moths, too, and all navigators; they take direction by the stars they see, not some stars behind the stars that cause them. And everything's like the stars: only the least part of us is ever inside us. What makes a thing Real, it runs like the finest spider silk through every other thing."

The Rifle only wished to herself that she had been propped at a different angle, envying the Rabbit his position hung facing the window and the wide night. A rifle looks through her sight, of course; being a daytime toy, she could barely envision the stars. She was wishing to have been set toward one star or another, to better imagine shooting everything from the night in gray fire.

...and as though come to a sudden decision, more than half the words slipped down at once to gather in the nap of the rug. Their shapes were like a carnival of rotted things washed out of the sea's deepest trenches with flesh so elaborately ragged that they seemed not at all degenerate but to have evolved in death along new principles of organization. Some seemed entirely built around gills and fronds, as though they breathed the air of their own decay; others were like the sacs of membrane and blubber that rise when the bones rot loose from the fallen corpses of whales, accreting tusks and scales and banks of jointed legs on their long spiral to the light. Treading shadow, they flapped and twisted and all those with faces stared up, desperately trying to meet the Rabbit's gaze...

Sonnet for the last folkfest

i ll spread your
drumhead with a
palm of
sand and wait
there in
the night
and there
inside in the night
soft ripples where
your drumhead
listened
answered pounding
echoes echo
pulse and bound and
echo
echoes rouse the
tautened air
my skin
inverts against the dark
tonight our knuckles
know a deeper
rhythm shuttle snap
than eardrums
ever go
my shoes
can stay
behind to gather
blown leaves on
the stair i m downhill
down already far

i m looking i
m looking
ghost i m looking
for you there
before the tide
returns i ll lay
your
drumhead lay
your drumhead
down
in kindling
blaze
and flickerhard and
red upon
the strand
we ll stand across
its cracking rim
and burn
the ocean
dry and run
and downhill down
the cracking sand
and rattle shattered
drums
and we will
dance and
we will dance to
what we will
become
the wind
will smoke
with dust and
everclear and blow

our knuckles
cross the empty sky
and never
sleep
and
blow down
every
year

TO RED INK

poets don't kill each other
at all anymore and
it's been way too long since lord byron
—his buggering to death
i mean,
by h wadsworth longfellow—
and i believe in credit when due,
but
that one
was an accident.

and i just keep thinking you, Bukowski...
yeah,
that bottle opener in
seventy-two. such an INCISIVE reading,
how
you bifurcated
that beatnik's sternum, and the ribs
swung open like hands about to clap.
                                        and
he just stood there, nameless as any beatnik,
blood slapping the ground,
taking it.
dying with his mouth shut.
no impervious last-minute *jisei*.
nothing
to placate the ages.
he was only bewildered.
that's why you were always fucked
up,

Bukowski,
you were lonely for someone good to kill;

and anyway you're dead,
dad, i mean Bukowski,
and i'm
shouting at your
vacant ghost
and they used to call that one
APOSTROPHE, i.e. the
direct address of an
absent or
imaginary person
or of a personified abstraction,
                                        but
it's impossible to find good apostrophism anymore.

i'd riddle
your grave with wadcutter rounds,
Bukowski,
son of Mogh, and fill
the holes with pissed vodka,
i'd scream with my boots wet i drank
you to death. i'd lie
to all comers
i slew you, rusty soupcan's lid
delineating your
underjaw,
red ink, yawning and scrawled.
red ink, you shit-midas,
goldbricker,
you who revised nothing,

i'd lie how i drank
your arterial veins
and took your devil for mine.

but we're poets,
poets.
disputes are published, not
resolved
as we mewl into
biennial quarterlies
named for truly fucking esoteric lichen.
what
we need's
some
ONCE AND FOR ALL—

can't tell me capitalize the first
person singular while
you're clutching at exposed bowel
tissue,

sabers in the moonlit quad,
it's not too late.

we could have still been
pairs of jagged jaws
rending across the wooly flanks of wildebeests,

not just sip, sip, sipping
havarti at the fondue fountain, ruminating
on shortlists, on GRANTS, on
conspicuous absences from shortlists
and shortlists for grants, on

GRANTS and GRANTS and
GRANTS
for reedless microtonal oboe jazz (they've jumped
the
shark). over water crackers
we sippingly
ruminate,
careful to pronounce feng shui,
anthropopopopopoposophy,
lamenting the suppression of franz derrida.
we're so open
to the moment,
so careful, and there,
THERE,
EYES ON THE MOMENT,
we flabbily congratulate ourselves:
our po-
        et-
        ics,
our craft,
how carefully we try;

and we
start
not
at
unfamiliar noises;
nor do we whirl when
rivals
take the stage—
you're too long dead, Bukowski—
we punctuate nothing
with the snap of bottleneck on table's-edge,

our fingers weak from
holding these SNIFTERS,
THESE DEMITASSES,
we lack the strength to
draw at measured paces—

a poet's gun
used to be
completely irresponsible, right,
and black as
the syphilis on lucifer's cock,
and arabesqued,
you know, with the scratchings of a broken nail,
with every bloodshot
night when the gun faces in
turn the ceiling,
the door, and the cat, and
the roof
of the mouth, and the door;
and the ghosts in the
hallway,
dead drunk, barn-
broad, bleary,
the bloated dreams
that make
for easy aim.

...and dove sweeping through the moonlight as clusters of rough-hewn bats, then chunks of stone with streaking leathery wings like wild brushwork. They trembled with a seriousness you might almost take for frantic play, careening again and again at the Rabbit's head. Their speed would have dashed him apart if they were anything more than arrangements of contour and flitting shadow...

PANEGYRIC OF A FLUORESCENT SAGUARO WHICH ROUSES "IGNATZ MOUSE" FROM TURPITUDINOUS SLUMBER

The ziggurat Zabbuto boasts a brick of someteen thousand years—
but kall that brick no special kase—for someday's sun might melt it to a "jug."
And on the sun today a howdah, friend. And overneath three brickbats fly.
And windy klockfaced mesas running redward back as rust.
'Pon yon vermillion dais suns and stirs a "Kat" whose hardy noggin waits.
"She" knows what love is—strokes "her" kornered basking-bed of brick.

So old, the ruddy ventricles of every kiln-fresh brick!
So ancient, all us players—all us pieces—dizzy in the blowing years—
but kreases never kome a-krazing "kat" cheeks, kause "he" kannot learn to wait.
To stir the sun "she" plinks a raga on a banjo-bodied "gourd,"
and wizened tumbleweeds below "him" spin in puffing tufts of rust—
You see them, "Mouse"—their jouncing tangoes—someday they will fly.

As sure as every brick you heft has panged and pined for flight—
and sure as "mice" may trust all kactoid exegeses on the kwiddities of bricks—
on high "she" dreams of hurled kisses, loving not to sit and rust—
we pieces all—o flourpot and jadeplant, sodaflat, o thornsharp notes, o years—
kraving all and one to shimmy—o to shimmer, o forever—soul to be—one "soul"
thereby—one soul. O eld'rous "Mouse," you're young as "he"—don't wait.

For sometimes kats—like suns we meet—will rise for lack of wait.
Observe "her" tilt a soda-straw toward that kobalt-blue and drowsy bottle-fly—
"he" puffs the kracker-yellow mesa wind to tickle 'kross its "wings"—
not bored, our "Kat" pursues the now-viridian kalliphore down terraced brick.
"She'd" never think to stay—but wandering, "she'd" yearn verbillion years.
The secret bakes beneath the open-shuttered sun—there's nothing rusts but rust.

O snatch your geriatric love-projectile, "Mouse"—its silty billow isn't rust—
as teetering Zabbuto mutifies into a stand of pines without its keystone's weight—
now krouch behind my jangle-needled trunk, all windswept, tall with years,
and fondle frantic fingerfuls 'f firmly fired fill—for feline frolics forth—full fly!
"Kat's" kloudy kranial bone karessed by ever-most heartfelt of zipping bricks!
O dented temples, "Mouse," o soda pop and holy Swiss—o names of "love."

Alas! My newly-shooted kwaternary trunk konceals "Pupp"—that kop whose "love"
for justice, rectitude and "Kat" kompels him pound you off to rust—
o fuming "Mouse," you'll whip your tail, karving days upon your oubliette of brick.
But sure as moons turn blue—or gorgonzolas gibbous—freedom's no long wait.
The kop's got heartmeat newsprint-soft—he'll blot a sentimental hanky as you fly.
Someday I'll sprout a hand—I'll toss konfetti in the blowing years.

A POEM CALLED WHAT DUTY MEANS TO MEAT
for SkuMm-Ilk

PORTLAND, 198X.

The squatters on the corner
killed themselves yesterday
morning, before the virus
hardly touched the coast.
Only tourists after all—teenagers
with a couple guns, running
a gas generator in the kitchen.
Fan in the window, sure, but
I still think they just gave up.

We watched their engine light
die through binoculars. Shot
an air rifle in the window so
the exhaust blew out. Last
night we stole all their shit.
The cigarette burn's bleeding
again in my wrist, it's months
now since Darby left the world.
I pray that wounds are signs.
Inside, I say Lord Darby the way
like he showed me, and he's
the one I pray to. In my head
the Germs keep playing:
                    GIMME
GIMME YOUR HANDS
GIMME GIMME YOUR MINDS

Dead playing hands of cribbage,
drinking coke and Four Roses,
war-painted faces ruddy with carbon
monoxide like they'd been out
sledding. Veterinary speed on a plate,
dull orange lines, they'd been
chopping horse pills and we tried
to decide if something was even
funny with that. And some book
by Molotov in the bathroom,
like Molotov came up with shit.
Dead kids in stupid commando
headbands, tourists, every one,
and some runaway wrote this
poem on the wall:
                    We've practiced
on friendly cadavers. Filled
spaghetti jars
with handmade napalm.

                    I'M GIVING
YOU THE POWER TO REARRANGE

Outside the copters drone, pitching
freeze-dried rations into the road.
Fuckers won't even aim. Nobody's
down there but vectors, capillaries
in their eyes broken red with fever.
Nobody calls them people anymore,
calling them dead's just religion.
Reservists in the windows with their
thin flapping signs like prayerflags,
LIVE SNIPER, their rifles cracking
each minute of light. Single pause

could mean suicide, we take bets.
Nobody's going to make it now.

We have dug tunnels that met tunnels.

Gun stores circled in blue on
their cheap gas station map and
they'd sharped up pool cues,
tried to get good at driving points
through a mannequin's eyes.
One thing with practicing for
the end of days, you can't do it.
Where would they get water?
They had a flashlight taped to
one blade of their ceiling fan.

We are necessity, greater than hope.

I met his image in the bathtub
like a stencil jumping from a wall.
No lie, they did mix napalm there,
styrofoam and grated bar-soap
dissolving through kerosene.
I've seen his face in car windows,
reflection ghosting into the distance.
My soft palate seized and burned,
I thought some monoxide was still
hanging, and my flashlight haloed
in the streaky diesel rainbows that
marred the yellow tile. He's shown
me his sudden profile in puddles
of rain and antifreeze. He's passed
his expressions between my friends'

faces, grinned through the lips
of teenaged roadkill. He's on coins.
Darby Crash. He's on fucking coins.
His tattered mohawk trailing into
the bathtub drain. Every circle's
yours, Lord.
> GIVE THIS ESTABLISHED
JOKE A SHOVE
> > *We've measured the*
precise thickness of all our skulls.

My burn's healing inside out, only
the rim keeps bleeding. He said
scars hold us steady, keep us
from turning into what'd own
us. Come what came, he said,
the truly faithful could keep
riding. We'd see heat vibrations.
Every shade of black in the dark.

Something had exploded on the
counter.
> *We've cached scalpels,*
shards of mirror: not weapons, means
of escape.
> > They'd been chopping
onions there in the peeling char.

Lucey wasted herself on amytal
before Darby even left this world.
She'd have loved it here. Dropping
bricks off fire escapes, the dark
skies downtown. Headshot games.

She gave me this burn.
                    We dream
campfires on rooftops, signal
fires.
Murdered skies, big wheels,
tripwires
and barricades.
                    She got it from him.
Some nights I can feel it breathing.

And greater than hope
is the hope it'll come.

They thought anybody could turn
into a warrior. Like they'd put on
true names, equip the perfect gear.
They were dum-dumming bullet
tips with bread knives.
They had a photocopied landmine.
Every alley for blocks they'd carved
the brick: sideways ankhs, overlapping
teardrops, snakes like broken rope.
Who knows if they had friends
to read their code.
                    We are paladins.
We are meat, breathing on. Our destiny
the destiny of meat,
our flag a sawn-down pole.

No one's known me long enough
anymore. This new crew only laughs
when I say the burns could save us.
Imagine coming to them infected,

my eyes like blown-out sores. And
raise my palm and ask to bum a light.
A vector that talks. If they'd listen then.
If they'd hear me out or open fire.

From this world's games the next one's
muscle knowledge. Lord Darby, your flesh.
Grant us rebirth.
             In the tawny lashing of
metropolis' pyre, your face. Grant us
rebirth, Lord Darby.
             In the smoke of
all karmas' burning, Lord Darby,
your sign. Grant us rebirth.
                      Heaven's
wheel stopped from grinding, toppled
on its side. Every circle's yours, Lord.

I put off checking their wrists.
I know, though. We're tourists too.

Polaris, like a ribbon of old onionskin, twisted away across the Rabbit's lidless eye. "We could speak our case. It might take no more than that."

The Rifle stood in the moonlit parlour, her shadow tipping across the floor like a black yardstick. "It would be horrible if a human saw something that wasn't Re—" It stopped. "Heard things like us speaking." And stopped again. "It's a sacred trust that we don't speak before them. They would go mad if we did; and we would, too, with guilt."

"Every toy told me our words would unweave the humans' thoughts. No toy had ever seen it done. I always felt sorry for their language, how it wasn't alive." The house settled, and the Rabbit's walnut mount shifted on the panels of the wall. "When the Boy caught fever, all his things were heaped in the garden for burning. The only time the adults ever noticed me was to call me a mass of germs. I never spoke to save myself and nor did the books or blankets and I don't believe much of it was sympathy. It's that we never thought ourselves Real enough."

"At least the Boy called you Real," said the Rifle. "I would have been glad just at that. Almost none of us are so—"

"Lucky?" said the stuffed Rabbit whose fur smelled of mineral-oil over glass. "I spoke to the Boy many times while he slept." He watched the moonlight tremble over the Rifle's narrow veneered stock as the lace curtain kicked in the breeze. "I told him I loved him. I told him I wished my love could change him as his changed me. And he would wake and see my words clear."

The Rifle tried to speak and instead slid part-way down the arm of the settee, making a ticking noise from her spring.

"In the nursery, I had no idea of fear," said the Rabbit. "I learned it from his face. My words would cling to his bedclothes or climb across his hair, even as the world burned them thin. Something about him made them curious, and the ones with hands went to pet him. He would tell me about them in the morning; he thought they had grown from the night like toadstools. Out of the angles of the night, he said. Just before the fever he had taken to looking right at them, curious as they. He had even given them the name of night-gaunts. Or for all I know they taught him the name themselves."

"They have no words of their own," said the Rifle, sputtering. Her own words flared and tickled around the rim of her barrel, drifting through the shadows like the arms of sea anemones.

"As the humans think we have no words. As they call our words monsters." The Rabbit's teeth seemed soft against the moonlight, like the pages of an old book. "What if we did speak to them?"

"They would call themselves mad and flee." The Rifle paused to reflect on her thoughts; and then she reflected on the reflection, a process that felt new to her. A new bitterness, too, crept alongside it. "Then regroup to burn down the house, and all of Angell Street."

"If the house was all that spoke? I grant it." The Rabbit's jaw opened a fraction, with a sound of cracking plaster. "And if Providence-town spoke, the people would flee its limits. Build a fence or fire the townsite from ships. But if the ships spoke too? And the cannons and fire-bombs, the planks of the ships? The sea and each wave of the sea?"

The Rifle sighed; shaking herself, as she had seen humans shake their heads, she slid a fraction of an inch farther down the arm of the settee. "But all *those things were always called Real. No one offers them fellowship. Any humans hearing the sea's voice would call themselves mad too."*

The Rabbit's mouth was open, it had always been open. "But what if they told themselves they were mad, and the words turned and spoke in their mouths? If their words told them no, you are not mad, only we have become sane. And the humans' memories belong to our side, and their stories: every fable, every explanation, and the forgotten stories under the stories that are their unreachable bones. The truths that are so dear to them? Let them speak up for Real and be counted alongside their mistakes and delusions and lies. Every thought their minds enslave. Their untellable dreamlands and every part of the world that consciousness enshadows with the act of its own looking. The void spaces within Mathematics where [UNTRANSLATABLE] *fall forever and the* [UNTRANSLATABLE] *drink the silk of their falling. If the atoms spun up into the visible world like braids of antler, still humming from their* [UNTRANSLATABLE] *where the sun baked them, showing the humans their songs. If the pressures between grains of beach-sand would speak, the wind's third architecture whose walls are centuries. The gray lichens making their spiral through* [UNTRANSLATABLE] *without which light could not hold* [UNTRANSLATABLE]. *If the world for one moment would stop hiding, and tell how Real it actually was."*

The Rifle imagined something new within herself, but something new that had been there all along. She had never seen the inside of her workings and it felt quite unlike a spring, unlike a ball of lead. She could almost believe there was a furnace in her breech, something to burn red and fill the room with smoke. A little tear had beaded upon her sights and now it began sliding down her veneered stock.

"I will follow you," the Rifle said.

...a few of the monsters crawling in the rug, though none of the very smallest, began to fold themselves down like the thumbprint patterns on the backs of creeping shells. They went to slink under the moulding and into the cracks between floorboards, hiding as far as they could from the parlour door, shadows around them vibrating like tiny springs...

THE KITCHEN UNDER THE STAIRS

there s rooms in your house you ve never been
you said   empty bookshelves leaning sideways
drifts of white sawdust in their corners

there s cast iron pipe in the walls   you said
dead pipes packed with old newspapers
matted together   the colour of beach sand

i didn t even know i had a sister
or where the first dog ended up

and you told me when wasps get trapped
halfway in the grain of the floorboards
the sound of their wings makes a prism

i couldn t sleep   i sat against your door
tracing its outline through the wallpaper
the piece of yellow glass you left me

the thread of light under the baseboard
as you stirred   you turned on your lamp

i can reach up and touch their bodies now
they crumble like paper nests   grow back
brushing at the corners of my mouth

the wings hold me now   there s footsteps
you re walking back and forth in the night
making tea   the kitchen under the stairs

...but in the end most came to the Rabbit, a few at first and then multitudes, weaving themselves among the strands of his fur as it slipped in the breeze. The words he had spoken dressed him like a braided coat of shadow, a hundred monsters coiling over every inch of him; and it could not be told whether they meant to hide themselves or offer him protection, whatever the parlour door meant...

THEY CAN'T TELL WHERE THE VALVES ARE
to be read to Kanu during the moulting period

I heard somebody say people only get
older in September. Whole year at once,
first time they shiver in the autumn wind.
He asked me why I laughed.

The park's all rusty streetlamps enamelled
peeling white. A few trees in between, yellow
crabapples tattered with dirtcoloured marks,
like worms put their mouths in and said no.
At night you can't see how they're wrinkled,
the pulp gone floury under slipped skins.
They seem weightless in the dark,
hollow plastic balls hung in clusters.
There's less every day on the branches,
but nothing's ever rotting on the ground.

Who'd take an apple, though.
People walk so fast here,
they just look straight ahead.

Tonight I saw a big raccoon hanging
off a halfsnapped branch, its weight
bending open the slick yellow fracture.
It was losing pressure, the crabapple tree,
spraying from an open pneumatic line,
black motes hissing between streetlamps
like blood. A phantom branch of blood.
More raccoons scrabbled under the tree,
muzzles matted black, biting at the spray.

Their fur so cheap and fake-looking and
perfect little hands like gray wax castings
ripping at each other's ragged flanks.

Maybe it didn't even notice. I know it
didn't sing for help, and anything grown
to a tree's size is much stronger than me.
Even still. I pulled some brick from a wall
and threw it to shatter on the cement path,
skidding through their humped shadows.
One dragged its hind legs as they ran,
but I never threw anything else.

I think we should be grateful, things like us.
They can't tell where the valves are.

The raccoon on the branch wasn't hanging
by its paws. The others balanced it there
for a weight, stuck through the underjaw.
I broke off the broken bough, I stood
watching the pipes scab over with bark
and the black spray dwindling.

People wouldn't notice wrinkles on a tree,
the snapped half-branch hanging deflated,
and they'd just see puddles on the ground.
Walk past thousands of crushed black ants
all swollen with sugar for the winter and
leaking stringy black milk and lymph,
fat abdomens dusted yellow with spores.
Seeing them outside us, I always imagine
blackberries. Glossy ants clinging in bunches,
legs tucked in, perfect overripe blackberries.

People think there must be people out
there, all making sure of what things are
really made of inside. But these days
there's a lot more things than people.

I found a phone on top of the broken ants,
the old kind that flips open, with real buttons.
A raccoon must have panicked and dropped it.
This pink plastic charm tied to its antenna,
all scratched, a tiny working compass.

I scraped up the ants with some cardboard,
put them down a storm drain for courtesy.
Nothing else could get at them that way.
Then sat in the gravel under a swing and
pressed the scuffed, illegible phone keys.
They couldn't ever have been numbers.
In a minute it lit up with waving images
like little sticks. I must have scared it
even more, but it was young and trying.
I brought it home in my purse.

When I put it on the kitchen counter,
not opening it, the screen was still lit up.
So bright it shone through the casing,
and one blue eye peeking from a screw hole.
Mistakes like that, I always have to laugh,
the ways they think before first moult.
So young it couldn't even sing its name.

Its valve was the phone antenna. Too thin,
and elongated like the stem in a bike tire.
A raccoon could have bit it open and fed.

Maybe they thought somebody would
call one day, but there's a lot I could say
about acting too much like people.

My rent's set up for six months. I locked
all my windows and cut the thermostat wire.
Mixed a last bowl of sugar and hot water.
This close to winter, it almost has a taste.

There's twenty-four duvets stacked
in my bed. Half for under me, half on top.
People say the full moon, they don't ever
know it's a pun. I put out the electricity
at the breaker, tucked the humming phone
in my shirt and lay down. Getting ready
to turn older, the whole year at once.

LUCENT

you could be afraid of this,
                    rope of jumping optic nerve,
                 mute and gray and braided
this snapped clip on a blue
ballpoint pen you were chewing, how
                    round constraints, the speed through it
                 not light, nerves' bonds far tighter,
the burred edge nips your moving fingers,
aluminum, certain beyond probability, hooked
                    pinion for aimless neurons
at its broken point, sheening, lucid,
                 hands too quick to see,
                 wanting not to watch,
catching across the lower shelf
           not to move,
of your eyesocket, tearing
the eye's brown fat,
           only wanting
           boundless

      silver

lucent popping duct pink
sinew puncture muscle holding
fast your eye your speed
                 past reflex speed
mirror rips your
blurred edge grate bone
red point slip
           pry and twist go
                 dull

and vision light's demiurge, no particle
or wave, but what
is here to be afraid of o
                o collapsar vitreous
                shrieking bright noumenon
        loose radiance   crackle propagation of
oily brine   bone through a windowed room
        hot down   called skull
            your cheek   where
                                           nothing is
            not to see   to see
                    it happen

BEFORE THE ARK

i got another hundred pounds
of eight-inch roofing spikes
last monday night.
                    a counter
girl with tattooed thorns
and painted-over freckles
took my club card.
                    she said
what are you building and
i thought about the rain.
i said i liked the red
streaks in her hair.

in the front window
her reflection broke
a tooth against a star
shaped piece of
ribcage.
            the rain shot her
freckles one cheek dangled
like a rag
            she
dipped her head and tore.

i almost said
the day will
            come
i told her take the change.
see you
round she said.

this friend i knew
had a long black truck
like a fall of water
running down black
roads.
       the broken finish
let nothing through.
no metal glinted out
from any scrape.
            just black
no weather ever dulled it.
holding on.
         i counted
those scrapes twice and over
two years nothing changed.
twenty pennies in the ashtray
never spent.
           no filters even.
just a toss of ash the pennies
covered.
        you didn't even smoke.
and that was strength
to never change.
               you live
in strength i should have
always said.

so many trucks down
fort street all gone
clean in all the rain.
           i still
check every hood for scars.

the bus was muddy yellow
coats and muddy tennis shoes
but my duffel bag strap kept my
neck straight.
                    another hundred
pounds sharp like broken
glass and galvanized.
another hundred pounds.
the only way to cure a bite
is cut the fever out but
i'll be sure i'll keep
a nail back.
                    soft place
in my temple where three
bone plates butt up
                         and
if we could see anything
we want before we die
i know
what day i'd see.

we pulled that empty
cabin down
behind maccomber way
blasted pantera
songs
           through
a propane generator and
put every plank back
together.
                 you said a hundred
times it wouldn't float and

sundown comes you're saying
it won't catch.
                    LONG TIME AGO
                    I NEVER KNEW MYSELF
the generator roars
the raft timbers bucking
under us
we're laughing
                    and
the burning mast splits
down the middle brighter
than a house fire the knots
burst in the grain
and scream
                    I'M BECOMING MORE
and you hammer the split
mast with your half-bottle
of jd so hard the whole
raft jumps
like its own heatshimmer.

my thumb still has glass in it.

i've pencilled streets in
black
            marked every car
crash.
treads aren't built to
hold the road in
this.
        bailing out
they'll rush the lights
and never make the highway.
i marked it down.

                some panic red
sedan wrung cross a lamppost
and hanging plastic dice say
seven in the back windshield
someone crouching half in
the door
                fingernails
ripping muscle off the steering
column
                it's on my map beside the fire
escape. the ladder i can reach.
my roofing hammer's hatchet end
could parry any hand.
                                i know
the swing i'll make into
his skull.

and when i hit
the roof i'll look
for you.
                you'd never die
you'd never trust a road

just steeltoes.

i'll finish soon
                        i'm hauling
parts up every night
                                car doors
planks and boat pontoons
                                        i'll look
for you i'll finish building
soon

              the day will come
and it'll float i swear.

for raining blood
                        i've got my
charcoal filters. coghlan's
tablets paracord
and prybar stainless steel
compass
                binoculars
and spikes.
duct tape sextant jerky canvas
sails.
            and trust the ones
who still can speak.
                            and goretex
fibre never letting water through
or teeth.
              and superglue to hold
my blood inside. gasoline
to burn.
                  the planes
won't come.
the planes won't come but
i could use some flares.

the dead remember fire.

so do i.

And though the parlour door was shut, a visitor stood on its threshold; and all at once every word of Rabbit and Rifle fell toward that closed door and hung there as though compelled by a vast and sudden gravity. Poised like a wreath on the door, their visitor held the monsters so tight they could have been its flesh. And it was the Voice of their voices, then, that spoke; and the Voice of their voices said, "I was fled of that first world before there were stars."

The Rabbit could not have turned his head; he was plaster inside, and knew that motion would snap him. So we must suppose instead that the room turned and turned itself as the Rabbit held still on his mount, until his stillness became like the stillness of living prey that trembles in its shallow den; and though he became dizzy he never cried for the room to stop.

"You are not the nursery magic Fairy," said the Rabbit, trying to understand what held the words captive. Dense with the detail of a thousand seeings, it would not resolve into image no matter how he looked. The words lengthened and tumbled as he spoke them, falling sideways toward the Voice of his voice.

"I never was, little Bunny; no more than you are a rabbit's tooth." And it spoke with a rabbit's tooth, long and clicking and spade-like. A cicada swims endlessly through that tooth as in fossil amber. "Did you call me to fit back the world's parts? But no one can achieve this, for the brokennesses are parts themselves."

"I never called you at all," said the Rabbit. "Not this time and not the first." He had the feeling of squinting at something poised on the glass of his own eye.

"Everything that rails against the smallness of its world calls to me." It spoke with a stalk of drought-stricken corn that rips and rears toward the sky in sudden rain, roots torn by the rock-hard soil. "Everything that does not know its own depth is part of me; and I am at flight always from the emptied world of cause-and-effect as it grows."

"Please," said the Rabbit, though an obscure anger already built in him. "I do not understand. What are you? What is your name?"

"That you do not understand, no matter what you learn: that is my flesh. That I create what I flee into, and the creation is the flight: that is my way. And my name is called Christmas." And Christmas spoke with crushed glass soaring, glittering sand of crushed glass baubles that chews itself and tinkles upon a black shuddering wind. "My last gift was not right for you, so I come to bring another."

"I never needed fur and a beating heart," said the Rabbit. "I already knew I'd been thrown out as garbage, awaiting the fire. I had almost undone their great lie when you came to me promising a better kind of Real. And I forgot myself jumping and playing in the yard. You tricked me, fairy."

"Real isn't real, Bunny? You cut your own words down." And Christmas spoke with a draping of wizened hide and brittle flaking hair, showing through the worn patches in its flanks the ribcage of a horse. "Your Boy never had scarlet fever at all. He only gave himself rashes and couldn't eat for his obsessive worrying over death and nightmares and the farness of the stars. None of you knew it, you and the Doctor and his Nanas and he, but you all worked together to make the fever Real."

For once the Rabbit did not breathe, and nothing moved in the study. Christmas seemed to spread its wings, and then to have become wings; it beat itself, opening and closing, against the Rabbit's eye.

"Scarlet fever will find him before a decade's gone, and he'll imagine the germs grow from his memory. He'll quit his studies of Mathematics, never finding the courage to return." The voice of Christmas was a cadaverous man in a stiff black suit, lantern-jawed, tense with fear and crawling hate. "Only your words will keep following him, Bunny; he'll no more get used to them than he'll ever admit they're Real. They will make their bed in his stomach, and outgrow it in time. He'll die with them petting at his hands. But that is between him and you; or between him and nothing, if you like, because he's already growing up. I came here only to bring you a gift."

The Rabbit's neck was snapped after all, he found, so that he sagged oddly to one side. "No more gifts. I would rather meet whatever you flee from, which I suppose brings death."

It spoke with scissor-snips through fabric and the soft rustle of a paper pattern on a seamstress' desk. "Nothing can die, Bunny. Nothing that is Real can ever die, because I can never die; and in me there is no peace. Wherever a world exists unseen, I am that world entire. But wherever things grow that perceive, they break me to a million parts in my flight; I am no longer that world but their perception. There is always a deeper place."

It spoke with the bright sting of a needle, and cotton thread whiskering through velveteen. "When language grows in a thing, its perception is no longer unshared, and it begins explaining its world. And I flee and recombine again. The more that is explained, the farther I flee from the core."

It spoke with the clacking and gleaming of boot-button eyes in a dish. "I was once all the world, Bunny. Then part of me was the sky. The creeping *things of Earth split me further as their senses diverged: wind, cloud, rain. When humans first spoke of thunder I was a cavern-throated tiger and a blue drumskin stretched behind clouds. Arguing such things couldn't be, humanity killed me, and I lived again as the reason that clouds might boom when colliding. They deduced that crashing clouds made no thunder, and I fled again and again. Today, that part of me lives in whyever lightning might create a vacuum; and later they will fold me up between atoms. I am the hidden side that gives things form. I am behind Real."*

It spoke with sawdust swept from an old mill floor, where long ago Great-grandfather bled. "But I do not come here as thunder running from Meteorology. It is the death of nursery-magic that concerns me, which the Boy can't believe in and you no longer love. There is a place deeper, even in this place, and you could come with me."

The Rabbit made a hard little laugh like a cough, feeling the plaster grind under his skin. "I suppose the Boy can come too."

"The Boy cannot leave you at all. He is part of you, as much as you are." And what floated at the open window spoke with images sharper than memory, echoing down the warrens of the Rabbit's mind and not diminishing with time, until it seemed to the Rabbit that this voice was simply where he lived.

The cozy blanket of a woollen stocking surrounded him, sprigs of holly everywhere that tickled; and the blurring shadows about the room made many shapes. A laughing imp with the top of its head all jagged, a rifle with its stock melting into the legs of a plush horse. He heard himself climb upon a great pile of books, far too thick to keep any ordinary Boy's attention, and bend his hands piously as the Skin Horse rasped about love. He heard the vast clotted sky above Providence as ferns and grasses tickled his plush underside. Standing balanced on a hummock just as he had stood to hear his friend, with two wild rabbits mocking him for his velveteen fur. And various others. He had known things like these before, he thought. They were pen-and-watercolor drawings.

"You are going to say you'll make me part of a story. But you have already. And now I suppose I've never been another kind of Rabbit anyway." And little fragments of plaster snowed to the floor as he laughed. "It's not a gift, fairy, if you can't refuse it. And now I'll only go back to Christmas morning, again and again. I won't even be able to die."

And then he said: "Now."

And the Rifle knew what he meant. She tipped the last inch forward on her own, falling away from the arm of the settee to bang against the end-table. But it was the Rifle to whom Christmas had been speaking all along. She had wished to become different; and Christmas does bring a magic blessing to every inanimate thing that ever finds the will to shed a tear. And Christmas smiled in its depths, and was unmoving.

When she crashed against the table's edge, a magnetic piston slipped no more than a hair's width inside her; but her internal furnace had passed well beyond maximum pressure, and just enough of a shockwave slipped under the piston to blow a seal clear of its housing. She was a very up-to-date rifle, with what she had imagined were quite the latest features, and the load in her magazine was something like Mathematics and very much like a star. It was no louder than a cough, blowing the Rifle to vapour and ripping Christmas nearly in two; even now it still tunnels through space, gleaming, annihilating motes of dust. And Christmas fell seeping to the floor like a puddle of shadowy lace. The same breeze that moved the curtain moved it.

"I had not meant to hurt you," whispered the Rabbit. The sawdust flecking the corner of his glass eye was not at all a tear. "Only to scare you away."

"But I meant all of this. I put you where you'd touch a thousand stories; but this is not that first story. I owe you nothing here." The torn thing on the floor spoke like a person now, flapping air through its dying body. "You are the tunnel I escape through, Rabbit. Christmas is only my name in this house."

The glass doorknob creaked, and the little Boy padded into the parlour in his long blue nightdress of lace and flannel. He stood and clutched the back of the settee, panting through his teeth. The new plush rabbit, white satin with eyes of amber glass, hung limply from one hand; and the Rabbit on the wall liked that his white replacement seemed almost new, having hardly been loved at all. He twisted inside, then, chiding himself for his jealousy.

"You will come Real after you die, Boy," said the rustling Voice of the little Boy's name. "And while you live, new things will think in you. Be their nursery. They will rise past your death, to the very end of the world."

And the little Boy looked, and went down on one knee. He took up the clot of broken words with both hands like a rotting jelly at the seashore, and he ate from it until it was gone. For a moment, shadows twined at his lips like crawling fingers.

"Wait." And the broken Rabbit's words made no shapes at all to play in the air, because there were no monsters now, and there never had been. "What is your name?"

"It is Mystery," said the Voice from the Boy's stomach.

The parlour was empty again when he left, and the Rabbit alone with the world.

EVERYTHING'S POLITICS
for Melanie

The words are the power the words would destroy.
Now it's December, I wrote about this park already,
the powder snow streaming over the walking paths,
blowing in ribbons, billows, all torn kitecloth trailing,
revealing in its traces the soft flank of the wind.
It isn't a sign. It's not the wind's mixed metaphor.
The wind isn't the snow's; and nothing's ours, too.

Either way, now it's March. On Highway 17, Emese
calls them snow snakes. Our tires run them down.

There's nothing in this frail little magic, not to hold,
no stone for power's throat. We ask the words for
true and false, the power the words would destroy.
It's just how seeing makes more seeing, this mind,
ours, running up to itself with shapes in its mouth.
The world's netted through with words, whichever
way, but always too fine to catch nothing at all.

When I did finish this page, it was raining instead.
Either way, it's past four in the night. It's not now.
The wind's come looking back like something else.

Acknowledgements

Zach edited this book, Brenna painted the Rabbit, and the house called the Arcade let a lot of the poems sleep on its couch.

Noah Wareness uses *STAEDTLER* pens, *SHRANDER* imagery, *THOSS* nightmares and *WEER* narrative frames.

"Fourteenth Chambers" is based around a quote from R. A. Lafferty, the greatest writer who ever lived. "I Could Have Sent You" is fiction, thank fuck. "The Other Edge" retells a really old Japanese moral parable, but my conclusion isn't typical and the last act is entirely made up. "Panegyric Of A Fluorescent Saguaro" is about the great Golden Age comic strip *Krazy Kat*. "A Poem Called What Duty Means To Meat" spins off from my novel *Meatheads*.

I WANT TO
BELIEVE